W9-BDV-528

Unashamed:
The Process of
Reconstruction

Richard L. Taylor

Copyright © 2012 by Richard L. Taylor Jr.

All rights reserved. This book or any portion thereof may not be reproduced or used in any manner whatsoever without the express written permission of the publisher, except for the use of brief quotations in a book review.

Cover design by: Jen Marquez
Jerry Jones: http://www.flickr.com/photos/skeletalmess/sets/

Paree Erica:
http://www.flickr.com/photos/pareeerica/sets/72157603745560 932/

Photographer: Bryson Martin

Visit Richard at www.unashamednation.com

Printed in the United States of America

CreateSpace, 2012
4900 LaCross Road
North Charleston, SC 29406
USA

ISBN 978-1481133975

CONTENTS

ACKNOWLEDGMENTS

Procrastination kills! I learned this firsthand while writing this book. The blueprint was designed in December 2009, but work did not begin until August 2012. I realized that talking about having a book that tells my story sounded good, but it was not something I had yet found myself committed to doing. Writing this book has been a very humbling and emotionally trying process. Nonetheless, as I reflect on the work that I put into this--my first book--I am happy that my completion came through my commitment.

This book was birthed through my experiences, good and bad. It's a book of blatant transparency, that I pray reaches the heart of your deepest issues and darkest secrets. This book was created for people who have ever struggled with their self-worth, or has been labeled as things other than what they felt they were. Each chapter speaks on a particular problem I dealt with or struggled to overcome, and is designed to show you that you are not alone. It is my desire that you can find as much healing reading this book as I did writing it.

I want to start off by thanking God for sparing my life and allowing me to survive two near-death experiences. I realize that I am where I am because of the Source! My faith has carried me this far and I know it will continue to lead me.

I must thank my friend, Ariana. You have sacrificed so much for us over the last year to see this vision come to fruition. Thank you for believing in me and trusting the vision I told you God has given me.

I would be remiss if I didn't thank my father and mother. I understand that you really did try your best to raise me in the right way, and you did. Despite our fights and disagreements, you have taught me so much along the way, and I truly thank you for that. Mom, your three sons are working hard so one day soon you'll be able to retire. Dad, I know you will never really sit down, but once mom retires, take a very long vacation--I'll watch the boys. I love you guys dearly.

To my brother Brandon, we understand each other on a totally different level than most. People always ask if we are twins and sometimes it honestly feels like that to me. You inspire me to be greater in everything I do. Your "hustle and flow" mentality is going to be what separates you from being average to being excellent in life. I love you twin! To my baby brother Bryan, I'm not putting any pressure on you, but you will be keeping up the banner of greatness years after Brandon and I. Know that I believe in you and I thank you for your drive to want to be better than the rest. I love you; keep raising the bar. To my two best friends, Cameron and Pierre--the two guys who literally picked me up back in 2009 and pushed me towards greatness--I love you guys. You have held me down continuously and I will do the same for you. Cam, the NFL is not ready to see you. Don't forget, make

God's name great and he will make yours great. Pierre, the only person who consistently called me during my morning run and on purpose, your wisdom and smarts will take you to places unimaginable. Pretty soon we will have our boat and it shall be called "The 3 Amigos."

I must thank my mentor, Quincy, for his constant belief in me as a life-changing speaker. When others doubted or weren't sure, you advocated for me with no hesitation. Like I always say, "If we had more guys like you, the generational gap wouldn't exist." This is just the beginning, Q. Everywhere I go I will be putting TRiO on my back. You saw me at an all-time low and allowed God to use you as a servant to help me. For that, I love you dearly man.

To my mother-in-law, thank you for always telling me that God did not make me ordinary! Those words stick with me on a daily basis, and I use them as motivation to conquer every feat. Thank you for always being so giving in everything that you do. Thank you for handing over your baby girl to me; she knows how to put up with me.

To all the men of my fraternity, Megiste Arete Christian Fraternity (Judah Chapter). Mighty Men of God Say! You guys have taught me the true definition of brotherhood and I am forever grateful. I love you guys more than words can ever explain--a bond like no other!

To my brothers Trent, Marquis, and Aaron; you have been a driving force in telling me to get focused on the vision God has given me. Every time you guys called, it was during a point where I felt like I didn't want to write anymore. Aaron and Trent, you were always willing to call and pray with me in a minute. Marquis, like you always tell me, "no pressure"--let's continue to impact lives through our stories. Also to my sister Delores, you always speak from a place led by God, never judging and always giving yourself even when you were drained from giving so much already...I love you.

To all of my supporters, I truly love you all. Your help and support with the "Getting Over The

Hump" series has been nothing short of incredible. I pray that you will continue to spread your stories and motivate others the way you say I do for you.

I have to thank my lovely Aunt Kathy, for her service in making sure this book is one of excellence. Auntie, you have always believed in me, and I thank you so much for that. I have always admired your keen eye for literature and grammar. Thank you so much for helping see this book to fruition. I can't wait to work with you on the next book! I love you!

A special thank you goes out to my production partners, who helped make this book possible. Mrs. Denise Bransford, Mr. Dennis Brown, Ms. Michelle Brumfield, Ms. Stacey Coleman, Mr. Michael Dozier, Mr. Armond Mosley, Ms. Brittney D. Odom, Ms. Jenna Plakut, Ms. Zenzile Powell, Ms. Chan C. Smith, and Mrs. Kim C. Taylor. You all have played such a pivotal role in ways unimaginable! Finally to my brother who is gone, but not forgotten, Steve R. Agee II. Steve, it is still hard to believe that you are gone from this earth. I want to thank you for being such a blessing to me during our time at NIU. To Mr. and Mrs. Agee, thank you for raising Steve to be the young man that he was. When people ask why I do what I do, one of the first people that come to mind is Steve. Every time I get on a stage, big or small, I close my eyes and bow my head for a moment, thinking of Steve. When my head comes back up, please believe that I am ready to blaze the audience because Steve is a part of my "why." I will continue to speak life to the masses as I strive to become the voice of the future and I will make sure to never let you guys down in this process. I love you dearly and I miss you so much bro--until we meet again in heaven.

INTRODUCTION

I have always felt misunderstood. I was a big people person and I kept a smile on despite the things I was going through. I never wanted to be perfect; I just didn't want to seem weak. As you read my story, you will see a side of me that you typically don't hear or see from a young black man. I wasn't a thug or a drug dealer or out on the streets. I grew up with both of my parents present in the same household. They provided for me, made sure that a roof stayed over my head, and that I was fed. You would think that my life was perfect, right? Well it wasn't.

While my parents are great people, just like any human, they made their fair share of mistakes. They weren't perfect, but neither was I. Some of my struggles were things that could have been considered attacks; others were things that I brought on myself. Either way, I struggled with many things, and they weren't the typical cliché struggles you'd see on TV or through media. My struggles were the taboo ones that many didn't want to discuss. Growing up was not easy, but I did it. I can say, I came, I saw, I conquered. Before I can tell you how, you must first know and understand the complexity of my problems and the problems of so many like myself.

CHAPTER 1: REJECTION

"Rejection is a challenge, set in place to test your ability to give up or keep going"
—Richard L. Taylor Jr.

Rejection comes in many different and unexpected forms. For some it comes through employment, opportunities, and relationships. For others, it might be a college letter or a school's athletic team passing on your talent. No matter what form you see or feel rejection, one thing is true for all of us--IT HURTS! The feeling plays tricks on our mind and causes us to shut down, sometimes from everyone around us.

I had experienced rejection several times in my life; however its impact reached a new level in

2006. Before this, I had my entire life mapped out and I knew nothing could derail my plans. I knew that I would one day be a professional football player. I knew that I would be going to college to play, and I would walk right into millions of dollars and never have to experience another day of financial worries.

Somehow, untimely heart problems ruined those plans, and I was crushed. My dream was snatched away from me and there was absolutely nothing I could do about it. I put so much time into football and felt like this was the only thing I had going for myself. I was tortured with thoughts of failure and wondered if I could ever really make something out of myself without football. I felt defeated.

During this time, I complained and moped about how unfair my life was and how I was a forgotten soul. However, I knew that I didn't want to stay defeated. I decided to give music a try again, as I used to sing during my childhood. In my mind I was determined to be a "star" somehow. It turns out that I was actually a really good singer, as I had begun to win awards and gain notoriety through choirs, musicals, and stage plays.

Despite my great ability in vocal performance, I still felt that my vision was only seen by me. The friends and family that I was hoping to get help from viewed it as a "pipe dream." While I understood the argument that they made about being able to make money after college, I was enraged that it was frowned upon and considered "not a real career." Over the next few months I tried to show just how good I was, but there wasn't much change from my support system.

This was my second experience with rejection concerning something I was so passionate about in less than a year's time. This resurrected my hurt from not being able to play football anymore. The only person that I felt understood me at the time was my girlfriend. Her support meant so much to me; but I questioned it at the time because in the eyes of our parents, it was merely puppy love.

When it was finally time for me to pick a college, I was elated after being accepted to Columbia College Chicago. I thought that this would be my chance to pursue a career in music, and prove to my parents that I was actually good at it. I had also gotten accepted to Northern Illinois University (NIU), which was my parents' first choice for me. Like any teenager adamant about something, I presented my dream to my parents again, but they just weren't convinced that this was a good idea.

My mom and dad felt that it was best for me to get out of Chicago and get away from my girlfriend at the time. I got into a heated argument with them about what college I would attend, and since they were footing the bill, I had no choice in the matter. I felt even more defeated than I had before and I completely shut down. Like many teens who feel like they aren't being heard or that life is unfair, I was filled with rage and anger. I didn't know how to deal with my anger, so I rehashed a bad habit that I started eight years prior--taking sharp objects and cutting myself, hoping that I could erase my mental and emotional pain with self-mutilation. I did this every day of my senior year, and it continued until I stepped foot on my college campus at NIU.

The rejection I felt from everyone around me led to a feeling of nothingness-- so much so I started rejecting myself. I walked onto this new campus not knowing many people, and not caring to either. I put on a great front, however, because I refused to let anyone see the real me. I felt like there was so much I had expressed that wasn't being heard by family and friends that I started to build this barrier against everyone around me. I even built this barrier with my girlfriend and our relationship ended shortly thereafter. This barrier got so strong that it led me to a place of distrust and envy. These feelings overtook my very being until I formed an attitude of resentment.

CHAPTER 2: RESENTMENT

"Resentment is like taking poison and waiting for the other person to die."
—*Malachy McCourt*

The resentment I developed grew heavily and quickly. When my resentment first hit, it was more of a mental attack; however, it quickly began to reflect in my actions as well. The first week of college was already underway, and I was determined to show my mother and father exactly how I felt about their rules and direction over my life.

I decided to put more effort and work into social clubs and parties, because in my mind if no one cared for me and what I wanted, then why should I care for myself? The second weekend of college, I decided to have my first major experience with alcohol. I connected with some upperclassmen and hit Greek Row. I ended up highly inebriated and having to sleep off a bad hangover, while regurgitating the lining of my stomach.

Despite the amount of pain I was in, I was determined to hurt my parents at all cost. I began to feel so cold and evil at times, and I found nothing wrong with it. I began to lose my desire for things that I had once felt so passionately about. Since I was no longer in a relationship, I thrived on trying to sleep with as many women as I possibly could.

This new lifestyle was a major change from what I was used to. Growing up, I had always aspired to be a different type of individual. However, I didn't always like being the outcast because of my experiences being bullied in the past. There was a time when I wanted to wait for marriage to have sex. I had never smoked nor drank and I always strived to be a positive example.

During my period of resentment, these goals quickly faded away.

Shortly after my first month of school, I got involved with a girl that I had been pursuing for a while. This relationship really didn't start off as a "boyfriend/girlfriend" type of relationship. I wanted sex, and I figured this girl would be an easy catch. We had a math class together, so I figured I would make my pass one day after class. I remember skipping out on the last 10 questions of my math exam on a Friday afternoon, just to chase her down and make my presence known.

She actually responded pretty well. I walked her all the way back to the dorm and we talked for a few hours. This experience seemed unreal because I found myself so intrigued by her appeal and flirtatious energy. I invited her to a party that my godsister was throwing that weekend. She accepted, and I knew that I was getting close. The next day came and we had a blast getting drunk and dancing our lives away.

Over the next week we spent more and more time together. That next Thursday night we had our first sexual encounter and I was sprung! I was so infatuated with her sexually that I missed all of my classes Friday to spend the entire day with her. By now I felt like I was ready to wife her, so that Saturday I asked her to make this official, and she said yes.

It was evident that I didn't care about what I was doing at that time, since I barely knew this girl and was somehow ready to lose it all for her. Mentally I felt a bad change coming along, but I didn't care to stop it. My habits of ditching class, having unprotected sex, eating, and being lazy were slowly catching up to me. Being sprung and having a careless attitude proved to be a very deadly combination. I stopped taking advice from friends and family and noticed instantaneous declines in my grades, health, and hygiene, and increase in my weight. Additionally, I developed a very bad spending problem.

As some of you may know, when you get to college you normally get a meal plan. This plan is one of your billed expenses and is normally paid with your financial aid. I remember having the Gold Plan which allowed me to spend $110 a week on food. For some reason that wasn't enough for me, as I ate through this plan in just a few short days. I not only used my meal plan on a daily basis, but I also spent at least $10 in cash daily on food as well. It wasn't like I had a lot of money in my bank account, but the money that I did have I blew through fast.

I was literally burning a hole in my parent's pocket, but I had this YOLO (you only live once) mentality. If mom and dad wanted me here, then this is how I would live my life. So whenever my account went into negative status (which it did often), I called my parents asking for more money. My resentment had reached an unimaginable level, as I carelessly spent money and started stealing. I had received a few warnings, but ignored them and almost got caught stealing. I was spending money on food and meaningless items, and repeating this cycle almost every week. I had gotten so good at something so wrong; and while I knew it was wrong, I could not fight the addiction and adrenaline rush. Other than sex, eating, and stealing, I developed a routine of nothingness.

CHAPTER 3: DEAD WEIGHT

"I, for one, hope that youth will again revolt and again demoralize the dead weight of conformity that now lies upon us."
—*Howard Mumford Jones*

My feelings and lifestyle of nothingness had consumed my everyday living. One of the more visible examples of my feelings of nothingness was my weight. I entered my freshman year of college still in my football frame at 205 lbs. No one told me that in college I would have the freedom to eat whatever I wanted, whenever I wanted, and in whatever quantity I wanted. The freshman 15 was nothing compared to what happened to me.

Due to my heart issues, I had not yet been released to work out or do any heavy physical training. My health and habits seemed to go from bad to worse, but I didn't care because I was actually enjoying "doing me" and not having to take care of myself. Growing up I always said that I would never be overweight. I was bullied back in grade school when I went through a chubby stage, and I remember never wanting to experience that again. Being called names like "fat ass" and "butterball," while getting my face punched in, was a very horrid experience. Since I was picked on because of my weight, I came home from school one day and thought "maybe they would like me if I was skinny." I took a butter knife and tried to cut into my stomach, somehow thinking that I would be able to extract body fat. This didn't work too well, but for some odd reason, I felt better about myself.

Little did I know, I had just started that habit of self-mutilation. I didn't cut myself for the next few years because I got a lot taller and I was playing basketball and football. After this happened, I began to get a little cocky in high school. It was like I had forgotten about everything that happened to me. I began to say hurtful slurs and make remarks towards people who were overweight. I treated them like they were less than human and didn't deserve to be on my level.

Now that I was finally in college, I guess karma had a way of creeping up on me. My mother always told me you reap what you sow, and when I got to college her words proved to be true. My not caring about what I ate ended up turning into a true gluttony problem. I was eating 4-5 big meals a day with no form of exercise in my life. Not only was I eating too much, all I consumed was junk and fatty foods.

As I stated earlier, I averaged $10 a day on food outside of my meal plan. I literally recall looking through bank statements and seeing nothing but fast food restaurant purchases from start to finish. I would eat entire pizzas by myself or 2-3 cheeseburgers at one time, and thought it was perfectly fine. Not only was my bank account changing week by week, but so was my body.

I wasn't thinking about myself enough to keep track of my weight. My girlfriend didn't seem to be bothered by it either, so it really wasn't a problem to me. However, my clothes were not fitting the same anymore--some were tight and others I couldn't even get inside of. Four months at school passed, and I came home for winter break at a much heavier 270 lbs. I hadn't realized that I put on the freshman 15-- times four --in a four-month span.

When I got home for break, I was ridiculed and talked about by family and friends alike. Since my parents have that "keep it real" type of attitude, they let whatever they wanted roll off their tongues. My father didn't hesitate to call me a "fat ass" when he was upset with me or wanted to discuss my weight. Going to family functions was the worst because I knew I could count on my dad to butt into a conversation with his famous, "Do you see how fat Richie has gotten?"

This did nothing but create a deeper resentment toward him. It wasn't just him though; former classmates and other family members had their fair share of words as well. Old friends would make my weight a topic of discussion publicly, saying how disgusting and unattractive I was. As much as I thought I didn't care, I started to realize that I did. I tried to shake it off and tell myself that I was normal, but was I?

CHAPTER 4: ROMANTIC ABUSE

"An intimate relationship does not banish loneliness. Only when we are comfortable with who we are can we truly function independently in a healthy way, can we truly function within a relationship."
—*Patricia Fry*

Going away to college definitely proved to have its pleasures. One of them for me was sowing my wild oats or "experimenting" with beings of the opposite sex. I broke up with my high school sweetheart because she had made it very clear that she was waiting for marriage to have sex. While I commended her for this, I had other plans in mind.

Before leaving for college, male figures in my life told me that my focus should be on having as much sex as possible, because that's what "real" men do. For a while, I thought they were right. I mean seriously, what better place is there to find sex than a town full of raging, hormonal young adults?

As I stated in an earlier chapter, being so sprung off of one sexual encounter started to show in my daily living. I quickly became a victim of the "do anything to please yourself" syndrome. When the young lady I was sexually involved with finally gave in to my attempts to be her man, all I could think about was how I could continue to experience this sexual euphoria. During this time, however, I developed a newfound relationship with God. This is important to mention because it made me a hypocrite to everything I was preaching on campus.

I did my best to keep my hypocrisy under wraps by lying and telling everyone that I was invincible and lust did not bother my girlfriend and me. I'm sure some people had their reservations about us and what we were doing, but I tried to push Jesus in everything I said and did. I'm not sure if it was from my resentment, or because I was just okay with the life that I had been living for the last few months.

In the previous chapter I talked about my drastic weight gain, and this relationship was a contributing factor. This young lady and I started putting on what I like to call "Cake Weight." This is the weight that some couples tend to put on when they eat together excessively. I really didn't think too much of the weight because of my newfound preoccupation with sex. In my mind, the only person I wanted was giving me what I wanted, and she didn't want much from me in return.

Since I was satisfied with the fact that my girlfriend didn't expect much from me I became somewhat of a zombie in my daily living, routinely ditching class and spending time with this girl. It has been said that "love is blind," and I was clearly the one on the blind end of the stick. Sex is a demon that will lure you with a sense of love and keep you from seeing the truths of things around you.

During the course of this relationship I didn't pay attention to any warning signs. We were about two months into the relationship when a few lies that my girlfriend told me were exposed. This happened during a trip with our school's gospel choir. I guess her level of conviction from the weekend led her to come clean about her sexual history. She had previously claimed that she was raped, but during the trip she felt obligated to let me know that it never happened. Somehow I was still so wrapped up in the sex that we were having, because everything she told me completely went over my head. I thought that maybe she was confessing all of this because she was truly falling in love with me. Not only was I oblivious to the fact that she had lied about her sexual experience, but shortly thereafter I received my first punch from her. I always called myself trying to give her the benefit of the doubt, by blaming myself for making her do it. The only problem was that during this time of me giving her the benefit, her attitude gradually got worse.

The slaps, hits, punches, kicks, and yelling became a regular occurrence. I had become the victim of physical and verbal abuse! Things in our relationship rapidly began to change. Every morning I woke up questioning who I would be waking up to that day. Would it be the girl I met at the beginning of the school year, or the person to whom I had become a punching bag?

Most days I was waking up to the mean and emotionally upset individual. However, because I was so whipped over the sex that we were having, I allowed myself to stay in this relationship for another year. During this year I noticed signs of possible infidelity, we were flunking classes, and I gained an even greater sense of carelessness in my life.

There were plenty of times I contemplated leaving, but I could never muster the strength to do it. I felt that I had become so physically unattractive that no one else would ever want me, not to mention the fact that I had been on academic probation for two semesters and on the verge of getting kicked out of school. Since I called myself being so close to God, I decided to pray and hope that a change would come eventually.

By my sophomore year, I had somehow developed a mindset that our relationship was OK and that all couples go through this. During that semester she hit me a few more times knowing that I wouldn't hit her back, but nothing compared to our last altercation in November 2007. This was truly a game changer for me, as this "beat the hell out of Richard fest" was like nothing I had ever experienced.

I was not perfect by any means, but I did try to keep a cool head, so I can honestly say that this fight was one sided. I had gotten fed up with her being so mean and I finally decided to confront her on her attitude. When I brought it to her attention she started yelling and tried to flip the script on me. I decided that it wasn't worth the argument, so I tried to let it go. She kept yelling and demanding that I finish "being a man" about my feelings. I didn't really say much and I think that's what upset her the most. At this moment I felt like I had no one or nothing to turn to for even a small bit of joy. I was having major issues with my family, my health was bad, and I couldn't find the energy to argue back.

She yelled and screamed, demanding that I talk to her and "man up." Everything seemed to be a blur while this happened. Minutes seemed like hours, as things got crazier and louder. By the end of this fight, her anger was evident all over my body. My shirt was torn, my body bloodied and scratched with whips, and my favorite watch had been thrown at my face while being called a "bitch" as she stormed out of the room.

All I could do was sit there and cry, asking "why me?" My roommate walked in later and asked what happened, but I couldn't murmur a single word. Tears flowed down my face as I cried in anger and rage. I began to contemplate how I had missed all the signs. I guess this is what happens when your mind is overcome by sex. I had gotten to a point where I felt like I deserved everything that had come my way. I told myself that this was the beginning of the end.

CHAPTER 5: FAMILY FAILURE

"Family problems come in all shapes and sizes;
some are short-lived and easily managed, while
others are more chronic and difficult to handle."
—*Unknown*

Being the eldest of three boys, I was expected to set an example for my younger brothers to follow. Now, my parents didn't know everything that was going on with me, but they knew something wasn't right. I was fortunate to have my father in my life and still married to my mother. My peers used to think that my life was a piece of cake, when in fact it was the complete opposite.

My parents were great, but they made mistakes just like everyone else. My dad is old school and has always had an "act first, think later" type of attitude. Being the firstborn, I always joked about being my parent's experimental child. I was chastised the most, I got the most whippings, and I was normally the one used as an example. This was all typical parent stuff that I didn't realize at the time.

Like most teenagers, I found myself trying to gain my own identity and place in life. Growing up as a young Black man with a father figure present is not as easy as some might think. My father and I seemed to clash constantly while I was in high school and college. A lot of our issues stemmed from the fact that he had his idea for my future and I had my own. Other issues were because of how I felt; like how I couldn't meet his standards because of who I was as a person.

During the process of figuring out who I was, I realized that things I liked, my dad didn't care too much for. I was actually scared to do certain things around him, like showing emotion or wearing certain colors, for fear that the words "weak" or "gay" would come out of his mouth. These were the little things that built my resentment. His "my way or no way" attitude also played a big part in the anger I had toward him.

Despite this anger toward my dad, I was happy at times because we were separated by 78 miles, and an hour and a half drive. During these times I felt like I was free from his ridicule and overly opinionated comments. Somehow, I forgot I still had to come home for holidays and school breaks. Of course...the first thing I had to encounter when I got back was criticism of my appearance and how sloppy I looked.

My parents claimed that they made these comments out of care and concern, but there is a certain way that concern feels, and in my mind this wasn't it. Being called a "lazy fat ass," or having to hear my father tell me that "I wasn't his son" and "I want my real son back," were not proper methods of motivation to me. As much as I was told to "be a man" or "man up," the fact of the matter is -- these words hurt! I am still human just like the next man, and it's only so many hurtful words a person can take.

The second contributing factor to my uneasy relationship with my parents was my failing grades in school. This was completely my fault and I had absolutely no defense. I knew that I wasn't always going to class, not studying, and not doing the assignments to help better my grades. My grades had started to slightly improve, but that didn't matter because I was still on academic probation, and could easily get kicked out of school.

Finally, my unhealthy romantic relationship topped the reasons why things went bad with my parents during college. In their eyes, that relationship was what was truly messing up my life. They might have been right, but I was so whipped that I was willing to defend it at all costs. Because of my willingness to defend myself and my relationship, and my father's "my way attitude, we fought pretty often. I was called names, kicked out of the house, and felt like I was not my father's son.

Granted, I played my part in the madness that was happening around me, but all I could think about was the heat that I was catching from every angle. I realized that I had a lot of hatred and anger built up toward my father, and I honestly wanted nothing to do with him. My mom always tried to be the mediator, but it didn't work too well. In my mind I knew that my father still viewed me as his "fuck up" child who disappointed him constantly.

During the winter break of 2007, I reflected on everything that had been going on in my life, and in my mind I felt like I could only depend on myself. I resented my family and hated being around them because of my father and how I hated him. I was the oldest son and I never seemed to set the right examples. This hurt me because my dad always made a point of letting it be known and in my mind this caused everybody to view me as the "family failure."

Section II

CHAPTER 6: NO WAY OUT

"The man who kills a man kills a man. The man who kills himself kills all men. As far as he is concerned, he wipes out the world."
—*G.K. Chesterton*

By the end of December 2007, I had gained roughly 105 lbs., and my GPA was below 2.0 for the third consecutive semester. So I was seriously on the verge of being booted out of school. Plus, my unhealthy romantic relationship was just as emotionally draining as my family relationship. I still decided to stay in this relationship however, because I didn't have the courage to leave. I was still being verbally and physically abused from time to time, and my identity seemed to be nonexistent.

Somehow I still managed to put on a smile and cover up all of my problems, while preparing for another semester of excuses and utter lack of concern for my future. The only things I had the slightest care for were singing in the choir and being with my girlfriend. Singing was my outlet and escape from my feelings. I knew that in just a few weeks I would be back with my choir family and singing, and back to a place where I felt like I could face reality.

Despite my lazy habits academically and physically, I still managed to hold a job. After all, as a broke college student, I needed some kind of income to sustain me. Since I worked for the University, I had to be back earlier than other students so I could get back to work. In no way, shape, or form was this exciting, but it was worth it because it meant that I was getting my freedom back. I was under the impression that my girlfriend was coming back to school early with me, but for some odd reason she decided to stay behind, saying she woke up late that morning. I didn't think too much of it at first and figured that I would see her in a week. Not even two days after I left, she started texting and calling me saying she thought we shouldn't be seeing each other at the moment.

"Excuse me? Where exactly is this coming from?" I asked. She didn't give me an answer that seemed even halfway logical or reasonable. Everything she said seemed to be pulled straight out of thin air. Mind you, I got this call late at night, and my heart dropped. I begged, cried, and pleaded for her to reconsider and stay. I guess my emasculated state of being made her feel bad enough to say, "Let's just take a small break." In my mind I was OK with that, because I felt like it gave me a fighting chance.

I still felt bitter and enraged during this time apart. I literally counted down the days until she got back. Somehow—miraculously—when she arrived back in town on Sunday, she said she missed me so much and wanted to be with me now. As broken as I was, I readily jumped back into the place where my comfort zone resided. I felt like everything was back to normal. The next week went by so smoothly and we even topped it off with a Friday night date.

That Saturday, we had our first below zero weekend of the year. This meant that most of the students on campus were cooped inside of their dorm room. My girlfriend and I lived in the same dormitory hall, on the same floor. We spent most of our time together and would do so that weekend. I didn't have a roommate anymore, so we spent the entire time in my room.

She got sick, so I took care of her while she rested in my room. We spent the weekend having good laughs, watching movies, and spending an abundance of money on food. It felt like we were actually in a really good spot with one another. By the time Monday came, I was happy because not only was she feeling better physically, but things really seemed to be back to normal.

That Monday happened to be Dr. Martin Luther King's birthday and, it would be on this day meant for "empowerment," that my life forever changed. Six o'clock rolled around and every ounce of "empowerment" was about to leave my body. My girlfriend finally went back to her room. An hour later, she called me, sounding pretty perky saying, "Hey babe, don't forget your hoodie is down here." I went to her room about 10 minutes later and her door was open. She was on the phone. I knocked, and she looked at me and said in a totally different tone, "Yeah G, yo' stuff is right there."

I looked at her sideways, trying to figure out exactly what had just happened. I knew something was up, so I came straight out and asked her, "Who are you stunting on the phone for?" She looked at me with a straight face and said, "My ex" (the same one she had broken up with to get with me). She said, "Before you start tripping, we are just friends."

In that instant it was like I had developed ESP, because everything made perfect sense now.

It was at this moment I realized that all of the "breaks" were for her to fool around with him. I guess in her mind, it wouldn't be cheating if we were separated. I stormed out of her room and raced back to mine. I sat there feeling angry, enraged, and incredibly embarrassed. I felt like I wanted out, but I was so overwhelmed that I didn't even know what out was.

All of the thoughts that raced through my mind were negative. The relationship with my parents sucked, my grades were horrible, and I was overweight. Now, the person I'd invested all of my time had been cheating on me for quite a while--the person I put it all on the line for, the person I turned away from friends and family for, the person I spent so much money on over the last year and a half, the person whom I, just a few weeks earlier, helped get reinstated back into the university. I yelled out as I cried, "I gave her everything, and she did this to me?"

At this moment I felt like a volcano, ready to erupt at any moment. In the midst of my tears I felt a darkness totally take me over. I grabbed a knife and a pair of scissors and stormed back to her room. We argued and more truths came out, but all the while she tried to defend her stance and her actions. I got fed up real fast with the conversation and completely tuned out her every word.

Overwhelmed with hurt and anger, with knife in hand I said, "If you don't give a fuck, then neither do I!" I then inflicted five quick, deep slashes across my left wrist--one for my pain, one for the mess she put me through, one for my insecurities, one for feeling like a failure, and the final one because I felt like I didn't want to live. This is what I'd done in the past when I felt like there was no way to escape my problems, but never to this magnitude. I ran back down to my room as fast as I could and slammed the door closed. Within a span of 20 minutes, police and paramedics were on the floor trying to stop the bleeding and get me to the hospital.

As we were leaving my floor, I remembered walking past her room as she looked at me in disgust as if I had done her so wrong. At the hospital it seemed like my life was flashing before my eyes. As I sat in the bed completely uncertain of my future, all I could do was think about how deep I had let myself fall. The pain from the stitches on my arm didn't compare to the pain in my mind and heart.

I sat there in agony and utter disgust with myself for what I'd done. All of a sudden a cloud of humiliation came over me as I realized I had to call my parents. The phone call was very brief, but that was just the start of my humiliation. Besides the obvious word of mouth, I knew that there was something else that would cause details of my incident to spread throughout the campus. I left the hospital the next day, and kept a low profile off campus at a friend's house. Due to the amount of blood I lost, and doctors being uncertain of my sanity, I was in the hospital those next two weeks more than I was at home.

CHAPTER 7: IDENTITY CRISIS

"For I know the plans I have for you," declares the Lord, "plans to prosper you and not to harm you, plans to give you hope and a future."
—Jeremiah 29:11

That next day I woke up and raced to find the school newspapers. What I read was one of the most emasculating things I had ever encountered. Almost every detail of my incident was in the "police beat" section. Not only was the story in the paper, but my ex had flipped the script on me and I looked like a complete psycho. For a brief moment, I didn't think about it because the doctor called and told me that I would have mandatory checkups for the next few weeks. They had to keep a close eye on my wrist because I had tapped the vein. "Richard you are blessed to be alive," were the last words that came out of his mouth. While this was very true, I wasn't thinking about how blessed I was. The only thing going through my mind was how I couldn't show my face on campus. No one really knew this, but I still struggled heavily with the thought of suicide for the next two weeks.

I was very unstable and confused about my position in life. I considered dropping out of school since I was already failing, but that wasn't a good idea. I was too afraid to go home and face my parents. It seemed like the only options I had were death, or being a man and tackling things head-on. I chose the latter. I received a few encouraging words from some individuals who were close to me at the time and it helped me realize that I had to swallow my fear. I did, and returned to campus that next week. Since I knew what I was up against I tried to keep a low profile.

My ex asked to be moved away from me, and was placed in a completely new dorm. I was prohibited from seeing her. My life felt like something straight out of a Lifetime movie. I say this because despite me being prohibited from seeing her, my ex would still make random trips to my room to "check" on me, and I was still falling into her web. Shortly thereafter I received a few threats and the cold shoulder by a lot of "supposed" friends.

It was obvious that my mind was completely warped by everything taking place. I played it cool, and decided to just go back to class and pray for a miracle. As that week came to a close, I received a call from my father. It was a Friday night. As soon as we got on the phone, I knew that this would be one of those "I talk and you listen" type of conversations. I was totally not in the mood for it, but I knew that this was going to eventually have to happen.

My father yelled at me for about ten minutes. He was telling me how weak-minded I was over a female and rambling on about who he thought I was. Although furious by his pure lack of understanding as to what I had been through, I didn't bother to put up a fight. I was mentally too weak to do so. This was a very rough night for me, because I felt like I had just made progress in my fight to get my head on straight. His words about me not being his son and me being weak hurt me in a way I hadn't experienced before.

The one thing that stood out to me in this conversation was that I did not know who I was as a person anymore, or what I was doing with my life. I was suffering from a true identity crisis. Even though my father's words hurt, one thing was very clear--I was determined to prove him wrong at all costs. I was fed up with him saying what I wasn't or what I would become. I had to prove that I was not a lost cause.

I decided that I would not go to see my family until I was an entirely new person. That plan failed due to an untimely shooting that took place at my school a few days later. I ended up rushing home and spending that next week with my parents and family. I anticipated an all-out war at home, but to my surprise, nothing like that took place.

This small vacation at home actually turned out to be a great time of reflection for me. I still had thoughts of proving everyone around me wrong, so I locked myself in my room and began to assess where I was in life. I had just attempted suicide, I was on the verge of getting kicked out of school, and I was an outcast to the majority of my peers. Plus, I had just been placed on probation by the university, and required to see a psychologist.

I sat back and created a plan of action that I felt would change my life forever. As I wrote what seemed to be an unrealistic plan, I doubted my personal ability to fulfill what I wrote. I lacked so much confidence and carried such a heavy load.

While I was in my room I came across a quote from Dr. Maya Angelou. The quote said, "Someone was hurt before you, wronged before you, hungry before you, frightened before you, beaten before you, humiliated before you, raped before you… yet, someone survived…you can do anything you choose to do."

This quote seemed like a slap in the face and it woke me up. So I looked back at the paper and told myself, I CAN DO THIS! There were three components that I felt would help me turn my life around. They were: *focus*, *discipline* and *information*. Focus was imperative for my mental state. It was the driving factor for how I approached every obstacle and test that came my way. Discipline was the trait that I needed to keep myself out of trouble and any situation that looked like trouble. Information would be the key to help me not only graduate from school, but to also step into a place of effective leadership.

Before I could do any of this, I had to be honest with myself about the place I was at in my life. I had to break the pattern of denial about what I had been going through and how it had affected me. I knew deep down in my heart that I was insecure, and my self-esteem was so low that I believed that I didn't deserve anything more. I felt like my weight made me atrocious to the eye and I wore the same clothes daily. My physical image was a reflection of how I depicted myself.

I knew that in order to change the way I felt and thought , I would have to change my ways. The only way this would happen was to apply the principles of focus and discipline from the inside out. In order for me to achieve what many would consider impossible, I had to recondition my way of thinking.

CHAPTER 8: THE TRANSITION

"Transition can be troublesome when you are climbing from the bottom up. The goal is to realize that the trouble in your transition is temporary."
—Richard L. Taylor Jr.

As I prepared to make my way back to campus after the shooting, I decided to go on a hiatus from activities and organizations on campus. I would spend my idle time on myself. I was determined to pass all of my classes and show that I was a stable person. I reevaluated my circle of friends and stayed as far away from my ex as possible. I told myself my life is only as much of a movie as I make it. This is where discipline played a major role in my life.

I got a call from one of my teachers asking me to come into his office. I rushed over and he informed that he had heard about everything that happened to me. I thought to myself "not this again," but he was actually caring. He told me straight up, "Rich, you made a mistake, but you're still a great person and I believe in you." Those words resonated with me as he told me that he was going to help me get back on track. He even trusted me enough to mentor one of his students and help her, even though I had my own issues.

Quincy had become my newfound mentor and he was very true to his word of helping me. He got me involved with the TRiO program, a nationally recognized program that caters to first generation college students, low income students, veterans, and people with disabilities. The reason why I say other TRiO participants identified with me is because we all had our fair share of problems and triumphs we had to conquer. I was very open with Quincy and told him, "This is the make or break semester for me, so let's make this happen." The next four months of school seemed to fly by.

I was actually participating in my classes and I noticed a bond began to form with different teachers. My mandatory therapy sessions were going very well and I think my "shrink" started to get the idea that I wasn't crazy at all. I felt myself gaining more confidence as the days went by. I was actually proud to say that for the first time in my college career, I was not nervous about my grades or what things would look like come May.

I spent a lot of sleepless nights in tutoring sessions, studying for every quiz, test, and exam. I started utilizing my teachers' office hours and seeking help when there was something I didn't understand. As the semester was nearing an end, I could boldly declare "I have given my all this time." The last week of school, I received a call from Quincy inviting me to an award banquet on campus. I didn't think much of it, so I changed my clothes and walked across the street to the student center.

While it was a great time and the food was good, I asked myself "Why am I here?" As the dinner came to a close, the award ceremony began and a few minutes later I had been called up for the 'Most Valuable Peer Mentor' award. I was shocked to hear my name being called for anything, but even more surprised at the specific honor I was given.

The fact that I was even capable of mentoring someone while I had my own problems was crazy to me. Apparently, I had made an impact on her during my time as her mentor. Her grades soared and she started taking command of her own personal issues. I was overwhelmed with joy when I found this out. I also won a $50 Target gift card. So in my mind, I was winning!

Back in my room, as I took in the events of the night, I decided to check and see if my grades were posted. Of course they were, and my mouth dropped as I scanned the list of grades and saw straight A's for the semester. While I was happy at the fact that I had a perfect GPA for the semester, I wasn't fully shocked that I had done so well.

I reflected on the hard work that I put in the entire semester. It was at that very moment that it clicked, "I'm off of academic probation." I knew that if I could put this amount of hard work into something and see this kind of result once, then I could definitely do it again. I felt so encouraged, I was even bold enough to commit to applying this method of hard work and sacrifice to every other part of my life.

I had finally gained my focus and I was determined not to go back to my former lifestyle. In a five-month span, I had another chance to attain my college degree and another chance at life. Over the next few years my life seemed to speed up. The transition from destruction to destiny had really begun to take place in my life. I decided to take classes during the next few summers and play catch up since I was behind from previous failures. It was as if I had "good luck" all over me during this time.

I started receiving promotions at work, I won a few service awards, and I started to gain courage as a leader. Granted, it took some time and even more service, but I was able to work my way from the bottom up. Due to my bad academic decisions the first three semesters, I knew I wasn't going to graduate in May 2010. So I determined that I wouldn't be walking across that stage no later than May 2011. I set realistic short-term goals and held myself accountable to them. During this transition period, it seemed that old problems had become old news. The only issue was that new problems began to take the place of my old ones.

I was entering my third year of college and I had no more elective--or easy--courses to take. The 2008-2009 school year was a reality check for me. I knew that I needed to pass every class since they all counted toward my major. No matter how hard the class or the teacher, one thing was for sure, if I wanted to walk across that stage I could not make any excuses from here on out.

I decided to do what most students would not do, in order to get what I needed. Some people call this is going above and beyond, I simply called it positioning myself. Sometimes failure comes from not being properly positioned or aligned in life, and I didn't want to fall into that category again. I went to every office hour and study session offered by each teacher throughout the entire year and made my name and face known.

There was a method behind why I was spending so much time with my teachers. The real secret was that I knew I was never a good test taker; even when I did study, the information never really resonated the way I needed it to. My plan was simple: do the homework, visit the teachers, and show that I genuinely cared about the course. This would make up for my weakness. I had discovered that only 4-5 students were consistently discussing their progress with teachers. This meant that when grading time came and my name popped up, instructors would remember me.

I also mastered the art of musical chairs in my classroom. What do you mean musical chairs? You might ask. This was college. It's actually quite simple. I noticed that in an overpopulated class of 300 people where white students were the dominant ethnicity, most black students sat in the nosebleed section. I, however, decided to sit directly in front of the teacher. I noticed that the teacher and the student were both misjudging one another in the classroom setting. What do I mean? You might wonder.

Typically, non-black professors viewed black students who sat in the back as having an utter lack of concern for the class. Yet black students normally sat in the back due to the intimidation of their new environment. These thought processes are pivotal in the grading and productivity of students in the classroom. So I decided to break this cycle and use it to my advantage. This turned out to be proof that it is essential to sometimes work smart and not hard in order to attain your goal. I utilized this technique all the way to graduation, and I am thoroughly convinced that it helped in ways unimaginable.

CHAPTER 9: THE ROAD TO REDEMPTION

"Understanding and tenderness would arise among us no matter how bad things got, and we found redemption in the very places we hurt most."
—Lin Jensen

During this transition, I knew that there were still some areas that I had yet to apply my principles. Sitting in the front of the class was merely the beginning. While this did teach me to work smarter rather than harder, unfortunately this couldn't be the case for everything. As it pertained to my weight, I was well over 330 lbs. The seriousness of being so heavy became clear when I got laryngitis in the fall of 2009 and went to the doctor.

What started off as a routine check quickly turned into a trip to the emergency room for excessively high blood pressure. When the ER doctor came in the room he told me that my blood pressure was basically at or beyond stroke level. He explained to me that despite my age, I was still at risk of dying if I didn't take precautions to lose weight and live a healthier lifestyle. For a moment I felt defeated, but I quickly reminded myself that I said I would apply greatness to every part of my life...no excuses. The doctors ran new tests on me to see if my heart was healthy enough to work out and they couldn't find anything wrong with it. This news made me realize that I could no longer make excuses about working out. This news also led me on a journey I was not prepared for.

The gym was one place I totally avoided the first three years of college. I was scared to step foot in there. But I recalled being in that emergency room and was quickly reminded that everything I hadn't done until this point didn't matter anymore.

The past is unchangeable, but my future wasn't. I got myself together and swallowed my anxiety.

My first time working out seemed like torture. I got on the treadmill and wanted to quit; I couldn't keep up for the life of me. I made excuses and decided to go play basketball instead. I randomly bumped into my mentor, Quincy, in the gym, and he told me "Rich, if you really want to lose weight you gotta get some real cardio training in." So I eventually went back to the treadmill and started at my own pace.

While my drive to lose weight was on point, my decisions on how to do it weren't always the best. I took my fair share of diet and weight loss pills, fully aware of the risk. I was totally uneducated on how to lose weight the right way, or at least that was my excuse. Truth be told, I was losing weight, but the results were minimal because of my desire to indulge in junk food all the time.

There are certain habits I developed during that time that I am not proud of. The worst was regurgitating my food after I ate it. While I felt good at the time that no weight was staying on, I didn't realize that I was messing up my body. I wasn't aware that this had become an addiction for me, and there was absolutely no discipline in my life as it pertained to saying no to the wrong foods.

I never really understood why I couldn't just break my bad eating habit in the first place. Due to my lack of self-control, I picked up another bad habit and this lasted for two years. While I was happy with my outwards appearance, I was angry at the fact that I was cheating myself out of my goal. It wasn't until after I graduated from college that I dropped this habit. It had gotten to a point where purging my food made me weak, fatigued, and dehydrated.

It was also very embarrassing hanging out with friends and constantly having to exit the room to go to the bathroom and throw up my food. I was tired of having to try and cover my tracks every time I was at someone else's house for a get-together.

Having to deal with thoughts like, *"What if somebody heard me or saw me?"* became too agonizing for me to deal with. I was tired of the constant guilt, and more importantly, I was tired of lying to the people closest to me who started to suspect something was wrong.

I thought that this redemption was going to be easier, but I was sadly mistaken. I knew that in order to see the results I wanted to see in my body, I was going to have to do things the right way. It was very hard to let go of bad eating habits and overeating. I had to learn how to discipline myself when I ate, and learn how and when to say "no." I came to the realization that this wasn't going to be a quick fix, but a serious lifestyle change—it is a process rather than a plan.

I exercised a new level of discipline and was conquering my fears, habits, doubts, and bad ways of living. Through this process, I saw things in my life fall even more into place. However, there were still some deeper emotional wounds that needed immediate attention. By this time I was close to achieving my goals. But before I could take the next steps, there was some true healing that needed to take place. Deep down inside I knew that I couldn't be a champion without revisiting and conquering some old chapters in my life.

CHAPTER 10: THE CONQUERER IN ME

"You can bury problems, issues, and heartbreak all you want. But if you're not healed from it, it will continuously resurface."
—*Richard L. Taylor Jr.*

During my transition, I made a vow to never allow my issues from the past to bother me again. I said that I would walk away from past hurt and pain, but this was a task easier said than done. I was fooling myself thinking that I would accomplish this without revisiting the very issues that led me to self-destruction. There were a few things and people that I needed to encounter face-to-face in order to truly walk into my confidence and freedom.

The first issue I needed to revisit was the relationship with my ex. I didn't need to see her, but I did need to address the things that she said and did to me during the year and a half we were together. This process of healing and letting go lasted for about three years. I blamed myself, however, for allowing the process to go on for so long.

In the latter part of 2008, I got back together with my high school sweetheart. While this was an awesome thing for me, I almost ruined it with my lack of willingness to deal with issues from the past relationship. As a result, I was steadily taking them out on my new girlfriend even though she had done absolutely nothing wrong. I knew that I messed up with my new girlfriend in times past and I didn't want to repeat this cycle, so I prayed. I asked God to help me deal with these feelings of self-hatred and low self-esteem. I couldn't risk losing her because of my prior experiences.

I've heard people say that prayer changes things. They might have been right because it was amazing to see the forms through which my healing came. I started to receive affirmation from people I once helped, my girlfriend, and my close circle of friends. I also started to take notice of all the greatness inside of me. Some healing took place during times of adversity, times where I had to act off of my ability. I truly appreciate these times because acting off of instinct forces you to see exactly what you are made of.

These actions were pivotal. I started to understand that, I might have hated certain things about myself, but those things were fixable. For too long I had been functioning in the mode and mindset of a victim. The problem with this is that victimization became my crutch whenever something happened to me. I didn't realize that I was actually supposed to use those moments as ammunition to go above and beyond whatever it was that was attacking me or hindering from greatness.

From revisiting the relationship with my ex, I started seeing myself as the man that I had been all along--one of courage, one that wasn't afraid to step outside the bounds of the social norm. I was the guy who smiles a lot and isn't gay for it. I wasn't a bad boyfriend; I wasn't a weak man, either. And just because I wasn't a "thug" or a "rough neck," didn't mean I wasn't strong. I wasn't a "bitch" like she once said. I was and had always been a man of a different breed, the type of man who could change the world with his unique abilities and mindset.

During this time, I read my Bible and prayed on a more consistent basis. I realized that despite what people might say or feel about it, the Bible was a great help and inspiration for me. I was able to discover some of my own issues and problems by reading through so many passages in this profound book. I also began to surround myself with the like-minded individuals. This is important if you truly expect to have success and truth around you.

My two best friends, Cam and Pierre, and my fraternity brother, Trent, were the guys I built the closest bond with during my last three years of college. I trusted and depended on these guys because they understood and never judged me. They were always brutally honest and didn't let me wallow in pity. This is what brotherhood and friendship is about. There's a passage in the Bible that says you will know a tree by the fruit it bears. If you ever want to figure out your "true" friends, analyze yourself and what lifestyle you are living.

In addition to those three friends, I also gained two father figures while in college. One was my mentor, Quincy, who was the key in my staying retained at NIU. I also had a spiritual father who we called Pastor Corey or P.C. P.C. was a guy who was bold enough to tell me about the greatness in me and even helped me realize things I didn't know about myself. It is said that you should always have a tight circle of people around you. This specific circle of men pushed me to face every issue that I'm talking about now.

The other issue that I had to revisit was the infamous two-headed monster, anger and rage. These were feelings I knew all too well for so many years. In today's society, a lot of youth are in mental bondage from anger and rage. What I've discovered is that this fury typically doesn't start within one's self, but actually stems from the family unit. For me, this meant that in order to deal with the anger and rage, I had to come face to face with another issue...my father.

I noticed that the men in my family all had very bad tempers when they got upset and were overly aggressive--as are a lot of men in the world. I knew that I had to deal with this on a personal level and make the choice not to act out in certain ways. I also had to get the hatred out of my heart and sit down and talk to my father. I didn't know exactly how to do that, so I talked to my mom about it first and she gave me some good advice, saying, "At the end of the day, you are going to have to just say 'dad, there are things that we need to discuss.'"

I knew this was important because not only was I about to walk across the stage, but I also was planning to propose to my girlfriend, and start a new chapter in my life. So in my mind all dead weight and extra baggage had to be removed. I took my mom's advice and I told my father we needed to talk. This was a very difficult conversation, because I knew that I would have to be vulnerable with my father in order to talk to him. For almost any man, this feat is challenging due to the amount of pride and resistance that we put up.

I am here to tell you that if you truly want to close the doors on anything that has hurt you, you will have to open yourself up and be vulnerable. Even though I was filled with rage, I didn't raise my voice. I told myself that sometimes in order to break the cycle you have to take the first step. I figured it would be pointless to yell because eventually no one would be heard and the "conversation" would go absolutely nowhere. During the process of my opening up, I cried as I let my guard down, and prayed that this would work better than screaming and swinging. I went into detail about certain things that were said and done, and I saw that my father didn't even realize he'd done some of those things. I believe now that my dad is getting older, his mentality has changed a little more. He was more receptive and actually apologized. I pointed out to him, that although he always told my brothers and me that we could come and talk to him, it seemed pointless when he would always outtalk us, and not really listen to what was being said. I continued explaining to him that more than anything else, I was hurt, and I had anger and resentment toward him that I didn't want to deal with anymore.

Surprisingly, my father immediately began to apologize and embrace my feelings the way I had always wanted. For the first time I felt understood by my father. It was as if a weight had been lifted from me and I felt so free. I told my father that I wanted to build our relationship and that I needed his help going into this next phase of my life. It was a refreshing feeling to have gotten that off of my chest. Yet, some people never do and die holding grudges.

The relationship with my father and I has grown tremendously since this time. As I have gotten older, I now understand the differences in the generations between my father and I. I didn't realize that certain tactics he used were tough love when I was younger. After we began to build the bond, I got a chance to see my father past my previous negative thoughts. I've come to the realization that we have so much in common from our likes, dislikes and mannerisms. Being bold enough to talk to my father showed me just how important communication is in any relationship. I started thinking about the issues that could have been avoided with proper communication.

I realized that it is imperative that we learn from these life lessons, in order for us to know what to be and what not to be. For me, I knew that I didn't want to hold onto this anger and rage, so I thought about how I could break this cycle for myself and one day for my children. I now consider my past hurts as motivation to help others who might have experienced similar situations. I learned that it's okay for us to be angry, but be angry with a focus that will create a change for the better.

A few weeks later, on May 14, 2011, I walked across the stage and graduated. I was filled with joy as I took in the moment and thought about what I had to go through to get here. I went from being labeled a "lost cause," an unstable suicide victim who was failing school and excessively overweight, to a college graduate with good academic standing, a clear knowledge of self and 130 lbs. smaller than I was 3 years before. Once I got off the stage I knew that everything I had been through wasn't just for me. It was for everyone who has struggled with something that could have potentially taken them out of this life.

CHAPTER 11: CLOSING THE DOOR ON YOUR PAST

Now that I use my story to empower those who have experienced setbacks, pain, rejection, and hindrances in life, my perspective has changed. I realized that different components of my story were helping people with their personal struggles. I've purposely been as transparent as possible in this book, because sometimes people don't tell enough. A lot of times we have writers and speakers that give thoughts, but aren't telling you one simple truth which is, *you are not alone*. You might be embarrassed about your past or current situations, but trust me when I say that you are not in this by yourself.

There are a few final points I want you to take from this book. The first one is that despite what you are going through, you are bigger than your problems and struggles. Cliché, right? But it's the honest-to-God truth. It might not seem like it during the moment you are going through such a hellacious battle, but you have the power to overcome any obstacle that comes your way. Remember that the strongest people are the ones who are tested with what seems to be unbearable problems. Regardless of what that problem might be, it provides a lesson and an opportunity for growth.

The second point is that there are others who are going through and will go through what you have experienced. You must realize that your life is worth more than a bottle of pills, a knife, a gun, a make-shift noose, and any other contraption that you would ever think of using to take yourself out. Suicide is something that isn't heavily talked about in the minority community, but trust me when I say it's a true silent killer. Somebody told me that if I take my life, then the person who is looking to take his or hers in the future won't have me there to stop him or her.

It's the exact same way with you! My life is a story just like yours, and your story is just as important as mine. People are going to need to hear your story to learn from your mistakes and for it to save their lives. You have to find and know your self-worth, because this will keep your mind from ever considering taking your own life. No matter what people might label you, or say that you are, it doesn't change who you truly are; you are a champion!

Since you are a champion, this third point is critical. Appreciate the process and don't run from hard work. Too many times we expect things to come quickly and easily; it's a natural human trait, but it's not the reality. You may sometimes have an idea or vision of doing something big like going to the pros in sports, or becoming a world leader. While these thoughts are great, the process of getting from where you are to where you are headed takes time. They take time for good reason, too. Maturation! In order for you to run that business, have that big load of money, play at the highest level, you need to know how to handle the pressure and the responsibility.

You can easily sit and argue about whether or not you're ready; trust me, I did it a lot, but the truth is, you're not. Understand that you can work smart--and I encourage you to--but some things only come through hard work and sacrifice. Remember what I said about the sleepless nights I endured to make my vision of graduating become a reality? Well you may have to do the same. You must be willing to assess what's really important in your life. *Do I skip out on the party at school or hanging out with the girls or the guys this week? Do I stay booed up with my significant other even though there is a paper I need to finish or an exam that I need to study for?*

These are the questions you must ask yourself in order to reach the goal you've set for yourself.

Remember that the time spent in between your present and your point of success is PREPARATION. You need it. So the less you fight it, the more you gain and the quicker success comes! The most important point that I will give you is to revisit past failures, people, and situations that hurt you in any way, shape, or form. Specifically, PEOPLE! My relationship with my father has improved since we had our talk, but more importantly, I improved. I'm here to tell you that if you deal with your past, improvement can happen the exact same way for you! You might have resentment toward your father or mother for things they've done and said. You might have anger and hatred for them not being there. Your anger might be toward a current spouse, or significant other. No matter who the person is, you must at least revisit those pains and acknowledge that they have happened, and there is nothing you can do to change them. Realize that you are not what they said you were, you are not what they label you, and you are a perfectly normal human being. You are capable of love and being loved, even if it's not from them.

This will allow you to walk in total freedom, but the choice is up to you. I've come to the conclusion that pain and suffering only exist as deeply and painfully as we allow it to. So, I encourage you to take control of your mind by empowering yourself to get past what has happened to you. This is a day-by-day process for some, but IT IS possible! You have a promising future waiting on you, so you can't allow these setbacks to keep you back. Stop allowing hurt to exist where it doesn't have to.

My final point for you is to live your life as boldly as possible. Appreciate yourself for being the individual that you are. Despite what people might say or think about you, you are the captain of your own ship. I am a firm believer and supporter of "saying the wrong thing to get to the right place!" Your bold character can cause global change for the better. It's the component that helps empower other future leaders and gives hope for the future. It's pointless for you to try and walk around like everyone else just to fit in.

Some people will love you and some won't, but that doesn't change the flow of your show. I encourage you to continue to be bold and courageous while "doing you." It's not everybody else's job to understand you and your specific skill set or creativity. Everyone won't get why you talk the way you do, look the way you do, or even think the way you do, but that's OK! It's people like you who others need to help them break free too. Never feel ashamed for being the individual that God created you to be; after all you were tailor-made in his image and likeness.